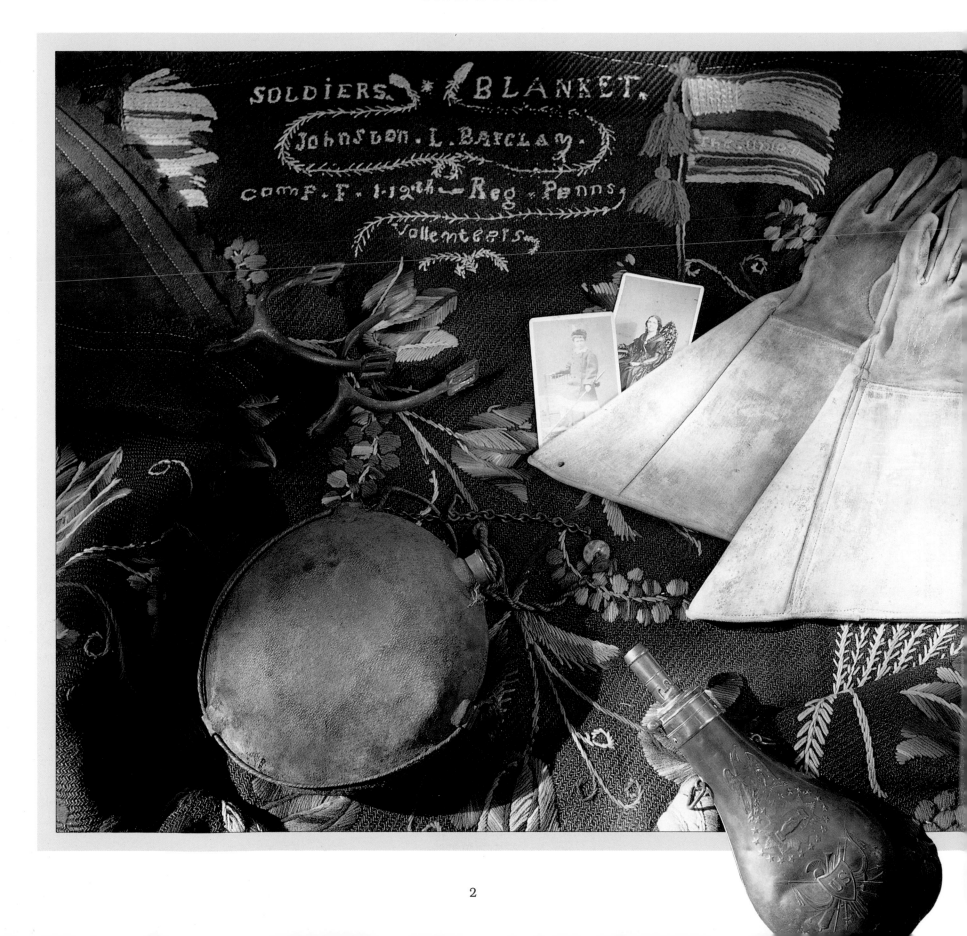

THE SOLDIERS
OF THE CIVIL WAR

WILLIAM C. DAVIS

Designed by Philip Clucas
Featuring the Photography of Tria Giovan

MALLARD PRESS
An imprint of BDD Promotional Book Company, Inc.,
666 Fifth Avenue, New York, N.Y. 10103.

Mallard Press and its accompanying duck logo are trademarks of
BDD Promotional Book Company, Inc. Registered in the U.S. Patent and Trademark Office.
CLB 2739
© 1993 Colour Library Books Ltd., Godalming, Surrey, England.
First published in the United States of America 1993 by The Mallard Press.
Printed and bound in Singapore by Kim Hup Lee.
All rights reserved
ISBN 0 7924 5557 6

MALLARD
PRESS

INTRODUCTION

When almost three million men, from North and South, left their homes and went off to war in 1861-1865, despite all the differences that made them fight each other, they had one thing in common. They were embarking upon the greatest experience of their lives. None of them ever had or ever would again live through anything like it. Farmboys who had never left their little villages and counties, and city men to whom the countryside was as foreign as the moon, were all suddenly thrust into a wider world than they had ever known, borne by their feet and their destiny to see America and live life to an extent none of them had dared imagine.

Their paths led them over the dusty, rutted backroads of half a continent, across rivers and streams and through country hamlets destined to achieve immortality thanks to their passing. Wherever the soldiers went they made history, so that more than a century and a quarter later, the greatest moment in the lives of a thousand places on the American map is still the day the armies came. But only when the armies came and stayed for a time did those fields and villages see the other side of Civil War soldiering, the life that the men led every day of the year except for those few that saw them in battle. This other life was the real story of Johnny Reb and Billy Yank.

A sampling of the soldiers' possessions. Carte de visite photos of loved ones, a canteen, a powder flask for a rifle, and a cavalryman's gauntlets, all lie on the most vital bit of all, a home-made blanket, this one belonging to a soldier of the 112th Pennsylvania Infantry.

CHAPTER ONE

GOING TO WAR

ABOVE: Johnny Clem, the "Drummer Boy of Shiloh," shows the youth they all shared.
FACING PAGE: Young men of the Sumter Light Guard at the outset.

There was nothing really sudden about the eruption of war in 1861. When the first guns fired on Fort Sumter on April 12, many had not really expected it, but few were really surprised. North and South had been bickering for two generations, with threats of coming to blows being made almost annually. Thus the young men of America did not have to face a sudden decision when the call to arms went forth after the first shots. They had had years to consider just what they would do, how they would act, on the day that talk turned to blows.

Thousands were already in uniform, members of the uncounted local militia companies, some publicly supported, others privately raised and funded by prominent citizens. Every state had its Home Guard or State Militia as well, and these, too, teemed with fresh-faced boys and enthusiastic, mature men.

Some came for no reason other than the uniform, the chance to parade on Sundays in colorful finery and to carry a big musket with a brightly-polished bayonet. Others answered the tocsin of war out of a spirit of adventure, a sense that this was the chance for a generation to see the country and do great deeds. Most were more serious, however, and in the end ideals of one kind or another put the majority of them into uniforms. The slavery issue accounted

4

for a number. Genuine antipathy towards the institution existed widely in the North, especially in New England, and many a Yank went off to war with abolition in his heart. Across the lines, a few Southerners went to war chiefly to preserve slavery, though only a few, for not one Confederate in a thousand actually has a personal stake in slavery.

Overwhelmingly, two other causes sent them to war. Northerners enlisted to preserve the Union against separatism, and to avenge the insult to the flag. And the men they were to fight enlisted for no other reason than simply to defend their hearths and Southern homeland from an invader. Those were the primary issues that impelled them to kill each other.

Whatever sent them, from the time they made their decision to go, Reb and Yank alike had much the same experience. They enlisted in small, informal companies in a local village, or went to their county

New York
Sept. 28th 1886

Mr. I. S. Reigart
Passaic
N. J.

This piece of flag is
from the original Storm-
flag of Fort Sumter S. C.
April 12 & 13th 1861.
Yours Truly
Peter Hart

FACING PAGE TOP: At the firing on Fort Sumter in 1861, all of them, North and South, were new to the business of armies and war. **FACING PAGE BOTTOM:** A typical Union camp scene in the early days of the war. These infantrymen sit before their wall tent, with a rude gutter before it to carry off the rain. Such shelter would be luxury by war's end. **LEFT:** The war produced millions of souvenirs, including this fragment of the storm flag flying over Fort Sumter when it was bombarded, and a letter attesting to its authenticity. **BELOW:** The letter writer was Peter Hart, who fired one of the first answering shots from Sumter.

Serg't Hart.
of Fort Sumter

THIRD IRISH REGIMENT

From Massachusetts, and First Irish Regiment for Nine Months' Service.

25 ABLE-BODIED MEN

raised to fill up the Company to be commanded by

CAPTAIN WILLIAMS,
Formerly of the MASS. 24th | now of the 55TH (IRISH) MASS. REG'T.

Come with us and our IRISH HERO,

CORCORAN

Let us carry the American Eagle over the Potomac down like an avalanche through the land of Dixie, recollecting

THE GLORY of the other IRISH REGIMENTS.

$150 Bounty

And all who enlist will receive the STATE AID.

All Recruits to this Regiment, on signing the Muster Roll, will go at once into comfortable quarters, and receive full rations of the best the market affords.

Captain WILLIAMS, or, Lieut. LEONARD!
No. 109 CAMBRIDGE STREET, BOSTON.

TOP: Yankee Militia parade on New York's Broadway in the days before the war. The busby hats would soon disappear.

ABOVE: Recruiting posters like this helped entice and excite hundreds of thousands to enlist.

towns, where the recruiting took on the aspects of a carnival, with marching bands, politicians exhorting their patriotism, and the young ladies waving their scarves and casting swooning eyes on those brave enough to step forward. Indeed, many a boy signed his name or made his mark on the recruiting sergeant's ledger solely because his girlfriend made him. "If a fellow wants to go with a girl now he had better enlist," confessed a pragmatic Indiana lad.

Mostly they were farmers, with a smattering of clerks, tradesmen, mechanics, teachers and the like to fill out their files. Eighty percent of them were under thirty, and some as young as thirteen, and even eleven, managed to slip into the ranks. They did so only because physical examinations consisted

of little more than a thump on the chest and a count to ensure that the proper number of extremities were present. It should come as no surprise, then, that several hundred women managed to enlist and pass examination, posing as men.

These perfunctory formalities concluded, the recruits raised their right hands and swore an oath of allegiance. They were in the army now. Their next step on the road to becoming soldiers was a trip to

FACING PAGE: One of the war's most poignant images is that of Private Edwin Jennison of Georgia, killed in the summer of 1862 when still little more than a boy.

FAR RIGHT: Private Francis E. Brownell of the 11th New York became an overnight Union hero when he killed a Rebel who shot Elmer Ellsworth for taking down a Rebel flag. The flag lies beneath Brownell's foot.

the rendezvous camp, probably nearby, where they got their first taste of rudimentary drill, saw themselves organized more formally into companies and regiments, and perhaps went through the uniquely American volunteer ritual of electing their officers. Soldiers elected their company leaders: lieutenants and a captain, and the company officers then elected the regimental commanders: major, lieutenant colonel, and colonel. If a prominent local

LEFT: Typical field gear for a Yankee sergeant, including belt with bayonet in scabbard, pouch for percussion caps, a shoulder belt, canteen, knapsack and haversack. **ABOVE:** The typical Confederate could be much less formal, like Georgia's "Racoon Roughs," who lent a colorful cast to Lee's army.

man happened to have funded the uniforms or weapons, or strained himself exceptionally to promote recruiting, he usually got the colonelcy for the asking.

Real training, however, did not come until the recruits were sent off to their camps of instruction, frequently in their state capitals like Camp Curtin in Harrisburg, Pennsylvania, or the host of camps that went up around Richmond, Virginia. However they went, by steamboat, train, or on the soles of their feet, they met a seemingly endless succession of waving crowds and proffered favors along the way. Few of them ever imagined they would kiss as many girls as they did on that brief trip to camp.

The euphoria turned to wearying drudgery all

too soon. "The first thing in the morning is drill," a recently arrived recruit wrote home during his first days in instruction camp. "Then drill, then drill again. Then drill, drill, a little more drill. Then drill, and lastly drill. Between drill, we drill and sometimes stop to eat a little and have roll-call." Most of them found it dreadfully confusing, not helped by being dragged out of bed at 5 a.m. or earlier and forced to attempt some evolutions even before their breakfast or the coming of daylight could help awaken their slumbering brains.

Thereafter, and for the rest of the day, their sergeants and officers kept at them constantly, bawling orders and shouting epithets and cursing when confusion inevitably ensued. None of these

ABOVE: Two friendly young Confederates reveal the chaos of Southern uniforms. Shoulder straps were not regulation, collar insignia were. One is gray, the other in blue, and their hats are non regulation.

ABOVE: A young cavalryman, probably a Confederate, proudly displays his saber and knife, both of them weapons he is likely never to use in battle.
ABOVE RIGHT: Members of New York's famous Irish Brigade show camp informality.

citizen-soldiers would ever become adept parade ground performers. If their leaders could simply get them from point A to point B without their stumbling over each other and getting lost, it was counted as a small victory. It did not help that a number of drill manuals were in use at the time, none agreeing entirely with the others, and when officers and men had been instructed from different books, conflict was inevitable.

The men studied and practiced squad drill, company, battalion, regimental, and even brigade drill, having to learn to recognize commands from voice, drum and bugle. Some manuals called for the memorizing of as many as 64 different trumpet calls. It became even worse when they tried it all while wearing heavy packs and carrying rifles that weighed almost ten pounds. And a soldier with a sharp bayonet at the muzzle of his gun could be a positive menace on the parade ground. More bayonet wounds were inflicted there on some hapless boy in the rank ahead, than in all the combats of the war.

Somehow, though, they got through the weeks of training, much of it perfunctory, especially in the early days when the rush was on to get men to the growing armies. Union General-in-Chief Winfield Scott tried to console one of his commanders in July 1861, before the first battles, saying "you are green, it is true; but they are green, also; you are all green alike." It was certainly true, but slim comfort to the tired, dusty boy who staggered off the parade ground every evening knowing that upon his hurried training, such as it was, might depend his life.

LEFT: The 4th Michigan infantrymen here show the frock coat at right, and the sack coat. Leggings did not last long, and the pistols were not at all regulation for foot soldiers.

ABOVE: Private Charles Pace of Company A, 18th Virginia Infantry, the "Danville Blues," wears one of the Militia uniforms that so many Rebels took to war with them. The shako hat, heavily "frogged" coatee, and white belting, were not at all suited for Civil War campaigning.

CHAPTER TWO

CAMP LIFE

ABOVE: Men of the 22d New York Infantry relax at their drums at Harpers Ferry in 1862.
FACING PAGE: Regulation Union drums from New York, Vermont, and Massachusetts regiments.

Whether at his camp of instruction, or later in the field itself, it was the home away from home that he thus returned to in the evening that he most remembered from his soldiering days. Johnny Reb and Billy Yank both proved terrible soldiers and magnificent fighting men, but they shone best of all when it came to making a life for themselves in their camps.

From the outset they had to leave behind them all their previous notions of what a "home" was like. There were no houses here, no bedrooms, usually not even four walls and a roof. In winter quarters, when the armies remained stationary for three months at a time, the soldiers might build rude log huts with fireplaces and chimneys, and even doors and windows, but for most of the year the common soldier lived and slept in his tent. They came in quite a variety, from the Sibleys, that looked like giant Indian tepees and slept twenty or more in perfect discomfort, down to the lowly "dog tent," made of two halves carried by individual soldiers and buttoned together at night.

Whatever sort of shelter he lived in, the soldier filled it with his few treasured possessions, literally all that he could carry with him in his knapsack or haversack, with perhaps a little extra brought along in the company wagon. Blankets, change of shirt

RIGHT: An 1864 image of winter quarters in Georgia, as General Sherman's "bummers" await the spring campaigning. Scavenged bricks and barrels form chimneys for "houses" made from tents, logs, and whatever else could be found. Many a Southern house found itself stripped to furnish and adorn Yankee huts.

BELOW: Passing the time in camp led to all manner of fun and horseplay, including shamming for the camera. In this case, it was the only swordplay these or any other soldiers were likely to see in the conflict. Their rifles would be their mainstay.

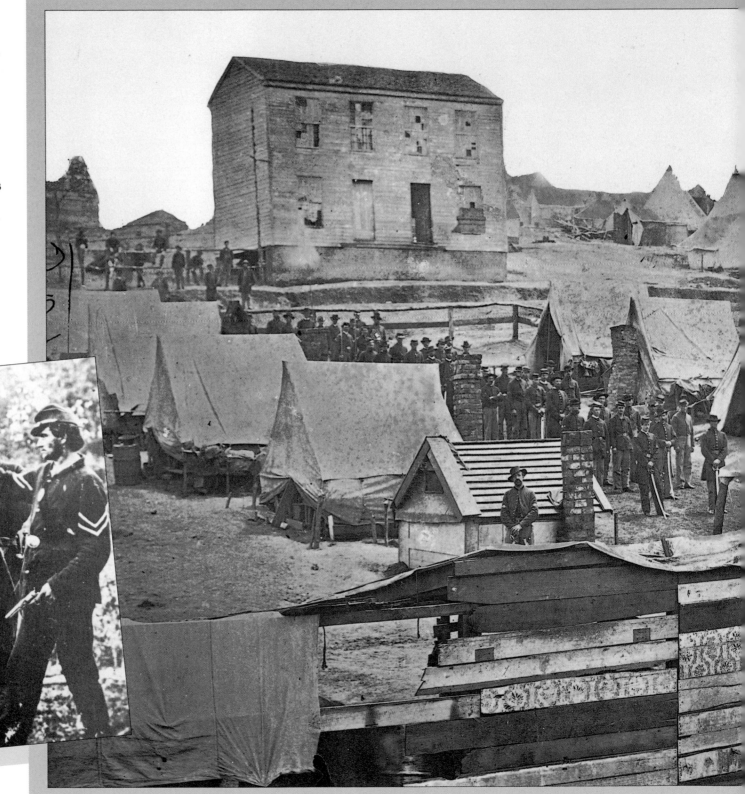

and socks, shaving gear, a Bible, a photograph, and a pitiful few other lowly bits of gear, were all he had.

Most treasured of all, for many, was their mess and cooking kit. It was not much – a frying pan, a coffee boiler perhaps, maybe a few tin plates and cups, with assorted bits of cutlery – but it was highly prized, so much so that in many camps soldiers planned raids on neighboring regiments to steal their cooking ware.

B-5419

It reflected the fact that the most important single event of the soldier's day was eating. Meals were what broke the tedium of drill or camp policing, the binding experience that brought the men together to relax, either from their labors on the field, or the perpetual boredom of inactivity between campaigns.

Not that what they ate gave them anything to look forward to. In both armies, by any standard, the rations were abominable. The staple of the soldier's diet was euphemistically called "army bread," though it was more generally known as

ABOVE: A lone corporal of the 22d New York poses before his tent at Harpers Ferry in 1862. Its sparse furnishings reveal the meager possessions that a soldier could keep. Even the camp stool was a luxury denied to most. This man probably has all of his vital belongings in the knapsack on his back.

INSET TOP LEFT: A soldier's few simple pleasures might include a candle to cast a feeble light for his pen, a briar pipe onto which he carved the names of his battles, tobacco, and a rude leather kit for sewing or writing materials. INSET LEFT: Mess gear included cutlery, a tin cup, perhaps a covered tin pot for cooking, and whatever was foraged on the way.

MAIN PICTURE: A typical camp scene in Virginia; a Yankee corporal and two sergeants play poker on a homemade table, while a drummer boy looks on. The open door leads into a rude winter hut of logs with a canvas roof. Searching for something to do to fill the endless winter days was a major pastime for men North and South.

FACING PAGE: Among the more photogenic of Union regiments, the 22d New York State Militia displays much of the typical Yankee camp gear. Inside the tent sits a cot, a stack of mess pots and pans, drying laundry, and more. Standard issue blankets air out on neighboring tents, while owners polish their bayonets, read newspapers, or take the sun.
LEFT: The less glamorous side of winter quarters, when rain and mud turned camps into miserable swamps. The "streets" are corduroyed with branches to escape the mire.
BELOW: The staple of the soldier's diet was bread, baked in huge batches by thousands of loaves a day. It was issued to soldiers by weight.

hardtack. The soldiers had other names for the three-to-four-inch square, half-inch thick, cracker or biscuit. They came so hard and unchewable that many called them "sheet-iron crackers" and "teeth-dullers." All too often, the hardtack came out of its packing box infested with vermin, leading to its nickname of "maggot hotels" and "worm castles." The soldiers beat them against rocks to knock out most of the inhabitants, then soaked them in water or crushed them under their rifle butts to make them chewable. Flavor was a consideration abandoned early on. To give them any taste at all, the men fried the lumpy, crushed bits in grease to make a hideous fatty mass they called "cush."

Grease was the other staple of their diets. No matter what they ate, it went into the skillet with a

RIGHT: In an era when personal hygiene was at best indifferent, soldiers in the field had little enough to keep themselves tidy. Soap, like the big bar at top right, could be made of lye and burn the skin. Tooth powders and paste were crude and abrasive. Toothbrushes lost their bristles easily, and straight razors lost their edge. Many men opted for beards instead. Combs were made from ivory, bone, or gutta-percha. The white cotton or linen towels were a genuine rarity, and all such sanitary items proved scarce after 1861, in the South they became almost collectors' items.

RIGHT: In the endless pursuit of entertainment, sports were a popular diversion, including the relatively young game of baseball. The walnut bat was used during the war, as was the leather ball. The red fireman's shirt is typical of the clothing worn by players, and the silver shield pin at upper right shows crossed bats. The photo is of George Muzzey, who played regularly at events like that in the handbill.

helping of lard or fat. Fresh vegetables were often in short supply, or else came in a dehydrated block of shreds that expanded prodigiously when placed in water. The men called them "desiccated" vegetables. Even worse was the meat ration. Only rarely was it fresh. More often it came as "pickled" beef or pork, preserved in a smelly brine, or else dried and heavily salted. "Bully beef," they called it, or "salt horse," or even "blue beef," thanks to its occasional color when the pickling failed to hold off the onset of putrefaction. Sometimes it arrived so glutinous from decomposition that the men joked about throwing it against trees to watch it stick and quiver. More than one company mess took a particularly evil meat ration and gave it a mock burial instead of eating it. No wonder that no farmer's field or livestock pen was safe when the armies were about. No wonder, too, that so many

TOP LEFT: An assortment of camp goods includes a coffee boiler, ladles and sieves, mess plates, a salt or sugar shaker, a combination knife-fork-spoon, tin cups, and a coffee bean roaster.

TOP RIGHT: To keep them dry, soldiers kept matches, or "locofocos," in metal match "safes" like the one at bottom. The straight razor is far more ornate than most, while the pocket corkscrew and pick shows much use.

LEFT: Officers and non-com's had more ornate finery, from epaulettes to belt sashes, and perhaps an album for carte de visites of members of the regiment.

men suffered almost continually from stomach and bowel disorders, thanks to the ponds of grease in which they cooked this rank mess to give it some flavor, or to hide the flavor it already had.

The best times came in the evenings, when all the drill was done. In summer, and on fall days especially, when the light lasted late, they sat around their tents or their fires and entertained themselves as have soldiers of all times. They wrote prodigiously, literally millions of letters and tens of thousands of diaries. Even the illiterate could pass the time by dictating a letter home to a more lettered comrade. Those who could read did so, devouring whatever they could find: newspapers, cheap novels, the Bible, political tracts, and sometimes even camp newspapers prepared and printed by fellow soldiers.

Almost every mess had at least one boy who could strum a guitar or banjo, or play a fiddle. Music echoed about the camps every night, and if most of it was not very good, still it lifted the hearts of the listeners. A few regiments even fielded small bands to entertain, often augmented by groups of amateur

FACING PAGE: Quiet moments in camp found those who could read studying letters from home, like the two at left, or writing in a diary, or just looking on and enjoying the interlude.
ABOVE: By contrast, men wanting more energetic entertainment staged theatricals and "stag" dances, with competition often keen.
LEFT: Every regiment had a few musicians, or even a band, to provide music for campfire and other entertainments. Some outfits even had glee clubs and debating societies.

INSET TOP LEFT: Smoking became one of the soldiers' chief pleasures, and tobacco a major commodity of trade between the armies. Cigars and pipes abounded, as did the ubiquitous match safes. INSET BOTTOM LEFT: Nothing suited a good smoke like a game of chance. Soldiers gambled incessantly at dice, cards - some printed with martial scenes - even chess. INSET BOTTOM RIGHT: The lowly coffee grinder gave them their favorite drink. MAIN PICTURE: Tobacco, cards, and beer or wine, made the ideal afternoon.

ABOVE: Women in the camps were not an uncommon sight. Many were wives of officers who joined their husbands during winter quarters or in garirson, like this lady with an Illinois battery at Chattanooga. During active campaigning, however, they stayed in the rear or went back home. Some with the armies acted as laundresses.

actors and glee clubs. One Kentucky Confederate brigade even had its own debating society. Hundreds of songs enjoyed popularity North and South, but one outshone them all, signifying the longing of the boys to return to their "Home, Sweet Home."

The rest of the time they took their fun where they could find it. In winter, a fresh snowfall was sure to produce snowball battles, some of epic proportions, like the one in the Army of Tennessee in March 1864, when whole divisions battled each other, taking prisoners and inflicting not a few wounds, all in the name of fun. They put on races and bet their meager pay on anything that would move, from cockroaches dropped onto heated plates, to men riding razorback hogs, or others pushing

comrades seated in wheelbarrows. They played baseball – already an old game by the time of the war – used cannon balls for bowling at ten-pins, and even dabbled in a rude variant of cricket. They whittled sticks, carved pipes from soapstone, mended their garments, stared at the evening skies and daydreamed, and most of all just sat around the coffee boiler and talked, fighting their old battles over and over again, and boasting of what they would do when they got their next crack at Reb or Yank.

Above everything else, they made friends, the kind of friendships that lasted for lifetimes, as they spent their youth and risked their lives on the battlefields of North and South.

LEFT: Some winter quarters were virtual cities, with populations of tens of thousands and cabins laid out in blocks along streets that were given names. This hut city in Virginia might have a library, a theater, and even a concert hall, all built of logs and canvas, and all destined to be abandoned with the coming of spring. Whole forests disappeared in the wake of the passing armies.

RIGHT: Winter huts being built at Fort Brady, Virginia in 1864 by the 1st Connecticut Heavy Artillery. The location on a downslope may come to be a curse when rain runs down the hillside, and into the huts. Still, it made homes, of a sort.

CHAPTER THREE

THE SOMBER SIDE

ABOVE: One of Illinois' monuments to her sons. **FACING PAGE INSET LEFT:** Americans would dot the landscape with memorials and (inset right) cemeteries. **OPPOSITE:** Rebel dead.

Few of these bright-faced young men anticipated the horrors that awaited them away from the battle-field, and fewer still ever suspected that their own camp habits more often than not exposed them to those dangers. Thanks to his hideous diet and inadequate camp sanitation, almost every soldier reported for sick call more than once during the war. Medicines were few and of little value, and some were actually dangerous, being based largely on opiates, arsenic, and lead. The cures were all too often more severe than the ills.

But worse still were the epidemics that swept through the armies. Never before had so many men congregated in so confined an area. Tens of thousands of rural boys had grown up without ever being exposed to ordinary childhood diseases. As a result, measles, mumps, chicken pox, scarlet fever, and more, killed thousands in the early months of the war. Typhoid and diphtheria, thanks to contaminated water, swept through whole regiments. By the end of the war, Yankee surgeons – the only ones who kept adequate records – determined that more than six million cases of illness had been treated, and those were just the ones that were reported. With something over a quarter million soldiers wearing the blue in the conflict, that meant that every soldier, on average,

went before a physician at least twice, and some repeatedly. They complained of loose bowels, scurvy, smallpox, pneumonia, rheumatism, and more. Typhoid killed at least 100,000, while dysentery accounted for even more of the 400,000 or more in blue and gray who died from germs rather than bullets.

But bullets, too, accounted for their share, and woe to the man struck by one of those gigantic missiles. When a lump of lead, varying from half to three-quarters of an inch thick and an inch long, slammed into a man's body it inflicted terrible damage. Often as not, the man was killed almost instantly, especially if struck in the head, neck, or upper torso. Otherwise, if the slug severed enough veins or arteries on its cruel path, a soldier could bleed to death before receiving aid, and even in spite of it given the crude means available for staunching bleeding. Surviving even that, he could die of simple shock.

FACING PAGE: Some of thousands of Confederate dead at Gettysburg in 1863. Burial details worked for weeks, and coffins had to be reserved for Union casualties.
ABOVE: Only the crudest of markers could be made for Rebel dead like these, most of whom would lie unidentified and lost.
LEFT: Other war dead lay in neat rows in places like Andersonville, Georgia, the prison camp that claimed the lives of thousands of captureed Federals.

SURGICAL STAFF.

Some argued that those who died outright were the lucky ones. For the rest, any torso or head wound was regarded as virtually untreatable. They were given whatever pain-killer was available, if available, and made as comfortable as possible. That was all. If they survived and healed, it was on their own, for military medicine could do nothing for them. More often than not, infection killed them if they survived everything else.

LEFT AND FACING PAGE: The green sash of a U.S. Army Surgeon, with his sword belt and shoulder straps of a lieutenant-colonel, showing the insignia of the Medical Corps. **INSET:** A Surgical Staff arm band.

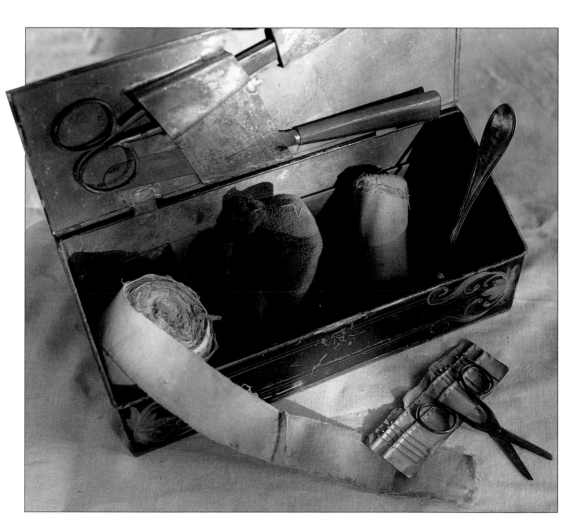

Arm and leg wounds were "treatable," however, and got priority at the field hospitals. A lucky man had a bullet pass through the fleshy part of an extremity, missing the bone altogether. With the entry and exit wounds stitched shut, he had a chance of relatively full recovery if gangrene did not set in. But when the projectile hit a bone, it shattered it, and almost the only known treatment was

ABOVE: Some of the apparatus most feared by soldiers – the bandages, and other implements used when men are wounded. Some were fortunate to have even these crude aids.

amputation. Indeed, even in flesh wounds where healing refused to take place, removing the limb was standard procedure.

In any such operation, there was no concept at all of asepsis or sterilization. Surgeons worked with filthy hands and instruments, passing millions of germs and infection from one patient to the next, and leading soldiers to agree with one boy who claimed that "hell will be Filde with do[c]tors ... when this war is over." Contrary to later popular myth, almost all amputations and other operations, even in the Confederacy, were performed under some form of general anaesthetic, usually laudanum. But this only postponed the pain, for recovery from amputations was long and traumatic, and treatable only with more laudanum or opiates. In many cases the pain and treatments lasted for years, and the decade after the Civil War saw more drug addiction in America than at any time until the post-World War II generations turned to it for recreation.

ABOVE: Union field ambulance men at practice removing wounded. In battle men often lay for hours waiting for attention. **RIGHT:** A field hospital and surgery at Gettysburg, with an amputation – probably staged – taking place. **FACING PAGE TOP:** Nurse Ann Bell tending Union wounded. **BOTTOM LEFT:** Yankee wounded in a field hospital in 1863. **CENTER:** A wounded boy not yet old enough to legally enlist. **BOTTOM RIGHT:** A home in South Carolina turned into a hospital for Union wounded. Hundreds of homes and warehouses had their floors stained with blood by the wounded of both sides.

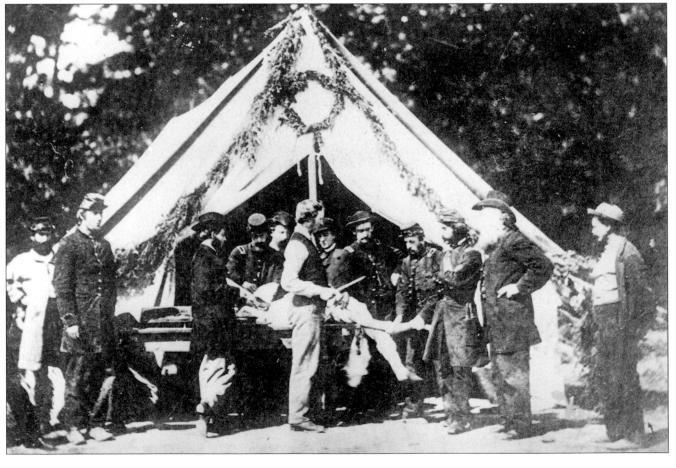

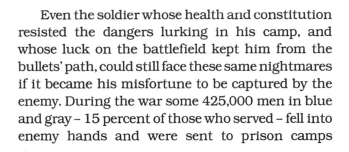

Even the soldier whose health and constitution resisted the dangers lurking in his camp, and whose luck on the battlefield kept him from the bullets' path, could still face these same nightmares if it became his misfortune to be captured by the enemy. During the war some 425,000 men in blue and gray – 15 percent of those who served – fell into enemy hands and were sent to prison camps

BELOW: Medicines of the era were crude at best, and a surgeon's pharmacy like this might consist chiefly of sulphur and opium and mercury compounds, many capable of more harm than good. Time did most of the healing.

scattered all across the continent. Contrary to post-war charges of cruelty and barbarism, there was little wilful mistreatment of prisoners on either side. The men suffered for the same reasons that they suffered in their own camps: bad hygiene, terrible nutrition, and exposure to the elements and the myriad germs that flourished in the rich human soup formed when up to 30,000 at a time were confined in the space of barely more than twenty acres.

In fact, most prisons soon became glorified hospitals. Andersonville boasted 33,000 inhabitants at one point, making it the fifth largest "city" in the Confederacy, and half its population was perpetually

FACING PAGE FAR LEFT: Like medieval instrument of torture, the surgeons' knives and saws struck terror in men's hearts.
ABOVE LEFT: Hospital stewards enjoying a drink. Many a medico sought too much solace in alcohol. **BELOW LEFT:** A Yankee field hospital after battle shows the results of bullets and surgeons' handiwork.

FACING PAGE TOP: A dread even greater than of injury or death for many soldiers was the thought of being captured by the enemy. Prison camps North and South were nightmares, as these Confederates captured in 1864 are about to learn. Many will not survive. FACING PAGE BOTTOM: Among the most notorious hellholes was Richmond's Libby Prison, where Yankee officers were kept. THIS PAGE FAR RIGHT: What a man could look like in time.

on the sick list. Northern compounds like Fort Delaware were only marginally better. Prisoners in the Confederacy suffered a harder lot only because everyone in the South was worse off than their Yankee counterparts. Rebel jailors fed and clothed their captives to almost the same standard as their own soldiers in the field, and in some of the more remote areas west of the Mississippi prisoners may

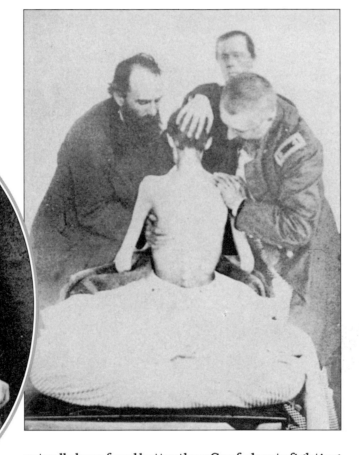

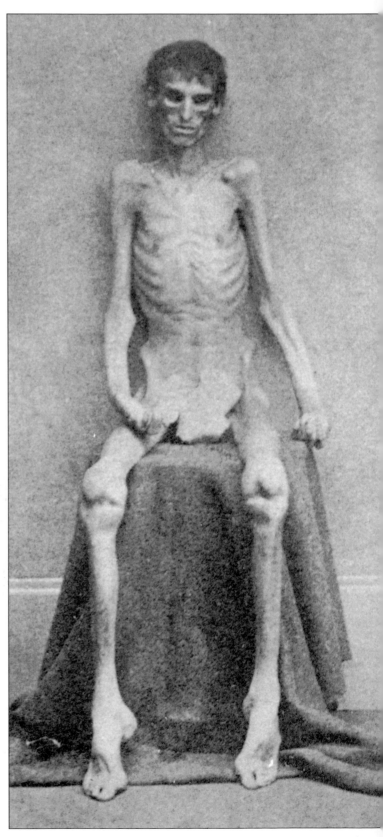

ABOVE: This poor Yank shows in his body the hardship of confinement at Andersonville in Georgia. ABOVE CENTER: Another Andersonville survivor being examined by army doctors, and apparently too weak to sit up unassisted.

actually have fared better than Confederate fighting men. In the Union, prisoners received generally much better fare, with more regular issues of clothing, blankets, and other necessities. Still, nutrition was poor, and the commissary general for prisoners of war, William Hoffman, rationalized that men leading a sedentary existence as captives needed less nourishment than active soldiers, and reduced their ration in 1863. It was not, again, intentional cruelty, but merely the ignorance of dietary needs shared by all men of the time, but Hoffman's action undoubtedly worsened the lot of thousands in his care.

Despite their hardships, the men in the prison compounds coped somehow, finding even humor and camaraderie in their misery. They told tall tales of the regiments of lice and bedbugs that shared their quarters, turned their gallows humor to betting on the number of dead at the end of each day, even made games of trapping mice and rats for extra food. To relieve the endless hours of boredom, they wrote and read, sang, and engaged in the perpetual idle speculation about release or exchange, most of which rumors proved to be cruelly unfounded. A very few put their minds to devising means of escape, either by tunneling, sneaking away from a work or wood-gathering detail outside the compound, or even hiding among the dead taken outside for burial. In the end, though a number of spectacular breakouts occurred, no more than one or two in a thousand ever successfully got away. The rest just sat, and waited, and endured.

THIS AND FACING PAGE: A large group of Confederate soldiers photographed just after their capture, the look of confusion and concern still evident in their faces. They have already heard horror stories of the prisons they are likely to be sent to. FACING PAGE INSET LEFT: The manacles were not often used on any but unruly prisoners. Nor did very many ever get their hands on keys like these, the brass one from Libby and the other from Beaufort, S.C. The hardtack at bottom right, however, was ubiquitous. FACING PAGE INSET RIGHT: To while away the time both in prison and out, men fashioned trinkets like these identity badges from bits of bone. THIS PAGE INSET BOTTOM LEFT: Prisoners were thrown on their own initiative to pass the time or entertain themselves. This watercolor by a Rebel at the Point Lookout, M.D., camp illustrates a minstrel show put on by his fellow prisoners. THIS PAGE INSET BOTTOM RIGHT: More than anything else, the prisoner worried about his stomach and keeping it filled. Rations were indifferent even at the best compounds, with starvation a possibility. The lowly hardtack, moldy, worm-infested, brittle, was still the soldier's friend.

CHAPTER FOUR

BETWEEN HEAVEN AND HELL

What sustained many a captive was the almost universal religion that pervaded the armies. Johnny Reb and Billy Yank came from a religious time and place, when the church played a major role not just spiritually but in society as well. Almost every regiment went to war with a chaplain, usually protestant except in predominantly Irish or European outfits where Catholics were most numerous. Even a few rabbis went to war, though soldiers often subordinated their individual denominations in order to attend whatever services were available. They met in the afternoons or evenings on Sundays, and when no chaplain was available an officer gave

the sermon, or even one of the men in the ranks. In the Army of Northern Virginia, General William N. Pendleton, chief of artillery, often reverted to his pre-war occupation by giving sermons, and in the Army of Tennessee several Rebel generals held forth from the pulpit. Stonewall Jackson himself sometimes spoke, but more often passed through the ranks handing out religious tracts.

Religious revivals twice swept through the Confederate forces, probably in response to the sense of desperation for their cause and the need for divine intervention. Most notable was the one that hit the Army of Tennessee in the winter of 1863-64, when services were held nightly

ABOVE: Chaplains like Thomas Scully fought for men's souls.
FACING PAGE: A pastor in battle.

BELOW: The wares of many a chaplain – glasses, crucifix, amulet, and a container for the holy Host. **BOTTOM RIGHT:** The United States Sanitary Commission passed out cups for soldiers' personal needs, and Bibles for their spirits.

throughout the army, with everyone from generals down to lowly privates participating. At least some of the impetus came from boredom; attending frequent services helped to pass the time, and some soldiers even took to rating the several chaplains according to their speaking merits. But mostly the interest came from genuine concern, and thousands were baptized in the fervor.

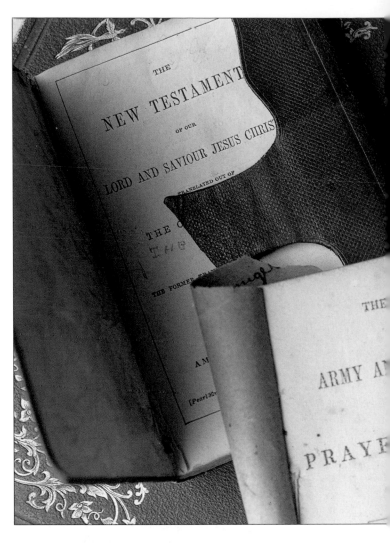

THIS AND FACING PAGE CENTER: The Sanitary and the United States Christian Commission distributed thousands of New Testaments and prayer books like these, though these are, in fact, Confederate publications sold or distributed by "relief" societies. **FACING PAGE FAR RIGHT:** A Yankee chaplain at his rude pulpit.

Special organizations North and South worked to further the ends of religion in the camps. The United States Christian Commission sent its agents throughout the Union armies, passing out Bibles, tracts and song sheets, providing wholesome reading matter of other kinds, conducting services in camps, and providing spiritual counseling to men who felt the need. The U.S. Sanitary Commission also did much the same work, though chiefly concentrating its efforts on day-to-day comforts for the men. In the South, a number of similar organizations did what they could, mostly on a state basis, like the Kentucky Relief Society.

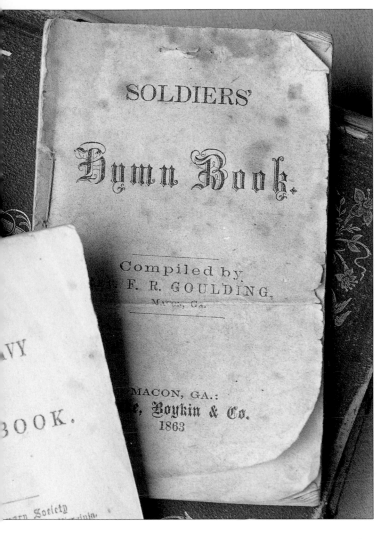

SOLDIERS'
Hymn Book.

Compiled by
F. R. GOULDING.
Macon, Ga.

MACON, GA.:
Boykin & Co.
1863

They had their work cut out for them, for maintaining the spiritual and physical morale of the Civil War soldier was a full-time job, and temptations lay at every turn. Most of these men had never been outside their home counties before, but now they were in the great, wide world, and in the company of tens of thousands of earthy, often rebellious, and very red-blooded fellow males.

Profanity was the least of their sins, and it prevailed at every level. Generals like Jubal Early and Joseph Hooker were reputed to "swear" their men into battle, while the lowly private soldiers brought with them from their homes every conceivable variety of oath, some wondrous for their inventiveness. While universally condemned, still it was a useful release for tension and frustration, and few soldiers ever suffered punishment for foul

BELOW: Chaplain Thomas Tipton's stern stare may betray the considerable battle that he and fellow ministers fought in trying to save men's souls from the degrading influences of army life.

RIGHT: The chaplain of New York's famous "fighting 69th" holds a Sunday Mass for men of the predominantly Catholic regiment. Colonel Michael Corcoran stands just left with arms folded, with other officers on either side of the improvised tent-chapel.

LEFT: Most of the men in Confederate and Union armies were Protestants, like these soldiers of the 49th Pennsylvania Infantry. Their minister, the tall man at right center, is Rev. Captain William Earnshal, a Methodist. His pulpit is simply two stacked drums. The regimental band stands nearby ready to accompany the men in hymns. BELOW: Quarters of the United States Sanitary Commission with the Army of the Potomac in Virginia in 1864. Its mission of health and spiritual care made it the precursor to the latter-day Red Cross.

language, unless they unwisely directed it to an officer's face. Behind their backs, officers were almost universal objects of some of the more ingenious epithets.

A soldier stepped onto more dangerous ground when he took a drink – or several. There was no official liquor ration in either army, though some regiments did occasionally dole out a tot to the men. But Reb and Yank alike showed remarkable resourcefulness in finding it on their own. Most of what they drank was of miserable quality, called "mean" whiskey as a rule, but often dubbed with more colorful nicknames like "Rock Me to Sleep, Mother," "Who Hit John," or "Bust-head" and "Rot of Pop-Skull."

The names said it all, and when a soldier took too much he was apt to perform all manners of infractions, from insubordination or insolence to an officer, to brawling, desertion, or worse. Some commanders believed that virtually all the ills

BELOW: The source of most misbehavior by soldiers was the bottle – or any of several bottles like these beer, wine, and spirits containers. The drink was often crudely made, and quite justifiably given a variety of epithets by the men who consumed it.

besetting discipline in the armies stemmed from drunkenness, and some took draconian measures to curb the vice. Medical stores of brandy and whiskey had to be kept under lock and guard. Towns under occupation sometimes saw their supplies of liquor confiscated, and in Richmond President Jefferson Davis threatened to banish alcohol from the city entirely if the merchants and officers could not control its access to the men in the ranks.

RIGHT AND FACING PAGE: Sometimes soldier misbehavior called for the ultimate penalty. Though this shows the execution of Andersonville Commandant Henry Wirz, any maximum sentence would look the same.

An inevitable concomitant to the rough comradeship of the bottle was gambling, and games of every sort were played in the camps, from endless varieties of poker, to "chuck-a-luck," keno, euchre, and more. Dice rolled across blankets turned into informal crap tables, and the men bet on everything imaginable, including cockfights. The officers tried continually to curtail gambling, but to no avail.

ABOVE: The offending soldier's fate lay in the hands of the court-martial, like this one sitting in New Hampshire in 1863. Sentences could vary from the humiliating and uncomfortable, like being bound to a wagon wheel (right) , to having to carry a ball and chain (facing page top left), or wearing a wooden barrel (facing page top right), or even being drummed out of the army with head shaved (facing page bottom), and sometimes branded according to the offense.

The story was the same with the illicit delights of the flesh. Camp followers and prostitutes appeared wherever the armies went, and in some of the major cities, especially Washington and Richmond, they openly flourished. For many a boy released from the inhibiting restraints of his home and community, such feminine temptations were too much to resist. As a result, rights over women provided further breaches of discipline, while venereal disease was rampant in some regiments.

For all of these offenses and more, the authorities meted out a variety of penalties, more in the nature of punishment for its own sake than out of any real hope that such treatments might actually act as inhibiting factors on the men's behavior. All punishments were humiliating, and most were painful as well. A spell in the guard house, confinement to quarters, rations of nothing but bread and water, were commonly used for minor infractions. A man could also be made to walk the

camps wearing a sign proclaiming his crime with words such as "I stole a skillet" or "Thief." Killing an animal without authorization might lead to wearing its skin for days, or carrying the carcass about.

More serious offenses resulted in wearing a ball and chain affixed to the ankle, or carrying a heavy log about camp for hours. Worse yet was riding a wooden "horse" or fence rail, and worse even than that was being tied spread-eagled to a wagon wheel for several hours, or being "bucked and gagged" – hands and ankles bound, seated on the ground with knees drawn up and a stick run under them and over the inside of the elbow. A man could be tied up by his thumbs, and in some cases even flogged. Cowardice in action could bring branding with a "C" on the forehead, and the worst crimes – murder, treason, desertion, rape – brought death by hanging or firing squad. It was not an era in which the wise man stepped too far over the line, for punishment could be swift and severe.

CHAPTER FIVE

THE TEST OF BATTLE

Red-blooded as they were, Yank and Reb alike, the soldiers in the ranks were, in the overwhelming majority, relatively law-abiding men when donned their uniforms to fight, not to make mischief. And when they fought, they could be magnificent. Throughout the history of warfare, the battle has been the ultimate moment of soldiering, the goal toward which all the rest – the training, the building of camaraderie and loyalty, even the fun and mischief – is directed. It was in the face of battle that these men found themselves, and showed the world who they were.

It was an almost indescribable time during the hours and then final moments leading up to firing the first shot and feeling the first heat of combat. "The feeling called *fear* did not enter my breast," a Tennessee Rebel wrote just after his first fight in May 1862, "but it was painful, nervous anxiety, a longing for action … and a dull feeling about the chest that made breathing difficult." Another Confederate, writing fitfully in his diary while marching toward the sound of the guns at Shiloh in April 1862, felt much the same. "I have the shakes badly," he confessed. "Oh how I wish I was a dwarf, just now, instead of a six-footer."

Indeed, whatever their fears in the weeks leading up to their first combat, almost all men found in the

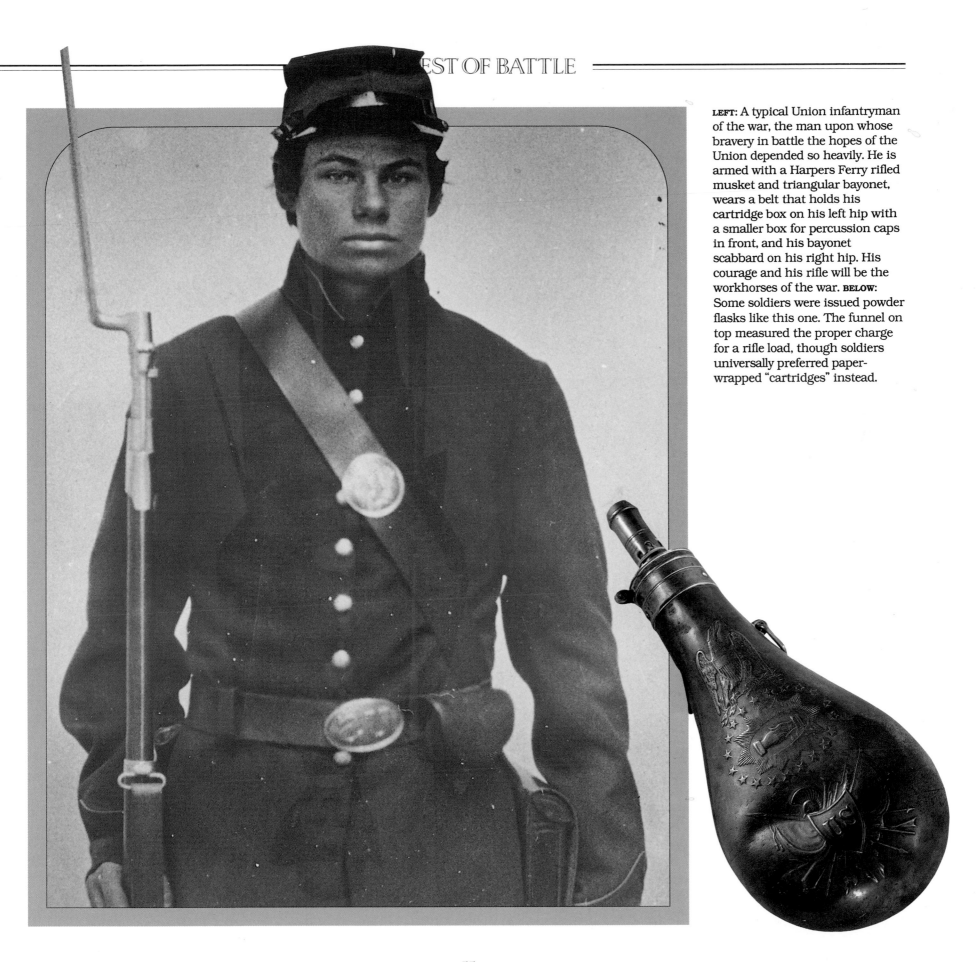

LEFT: A typical Union infantryman of the war, the man upon whose bravery in battle the hopes of the Union depended so heavily. He is armed with a Harpers Ferry rifled musket and triangular bayonet, wears a belt that holds his cartridge box on his left hip with a smaller box for percussion caps in front, and his bayonet scabbard on his right hip. His courage and his rifle will be the workhorses of the war. **BELOW:** Some soldiers were issued powder flasks like this one. The funnel on top measured the proper charge for a rifle load, though soldiers universally preferred paper-wrapped "cartridges" instead.

ABOVE: Many thousands of Yankees sat out much of the war in garrisons behind the line, or, like these men of a heavy artillery unit, serving in one of the dozens of forts ringing Washington and other cities deemed vulnerable to Confederate attack. Except during a July 1864 raid by Jubal Early's corps, these soldiers and their rifles and cannon may have gone through the war without firing a shot. FACING PAGE BOTTOM: A Yankee artillery battery of Parrott rifles in formation for battle in Virginia. Ammunition carriages stand behind the guns and further caissons at the rear.

end that, instead of terror at the last moment, they felt a crushing anxiety to get into the fight, a hurry to get it started and done with, perhaps because it meant that all the long waiting would finally be over.

"With your first shot you become a new man," said a Confederate who himself became a "new man" at the First Battle of Bull Run. "Fear has no existence in your bosom. Hesitation gives way to an uncontrollable desire to rush into the thickest of the fight." A first-timer on the other side of the line found the same thing. "After the first round the fear left me," wrote this Billy Yank, "and I was as cool as ever I was in my life."

That first shot was an experience that bound them all to a fraternity stronger than all the issues that divided them. Early on the morning of battle the drums and bugles awakened them – assuming they had been able to sleep, that is, for no battle came as a surprise, and most men, veterans and neophytes alike, spent fitful evenings before a battle,

many writing what they feared to be their last letters home, or putting their names and addresses on slips of paper tucked into their pockets so that, if killed, they could be identified and their bodies sent home. Once awakened, the soldier ate a hurried breakfast if there was time, or more likely gulped some coffee and crunched on a hardtack while rushing to his place in the column.

By dawn, the cannon fire and skirmishers' peppering away could probably be heard a few miles ahead. The men fell in line. "I can never forget my thoughts as I stood there and looked around," wrote a Tennessean in 1862. He looked around at his comrades, some boys he had known since youth, and realized for the first time that in a few hours time some of them might be dead. He watched as they made sorry attempts to jest and be jaunty, knowing that they felt the same fear as he did. Curiously, right in those moments, the fear that men felt was not of pain and death, but that they would turn coward and run in front of their braver

fellows. "I am afraid that the groans of the wounded & dying will make me shake," confessed one Federal, while a Rebel boy admitted after his first fight that "though i did not run i mite have run if i had thought of it in time."

Rapidly the men marched to the sound of the guns. Then they were halted somewhere behind the battle line while their officers got their orders. These were the worst moments of all. Mouths dry, palms sweaty, they clung to the ground, checked to make certain their bayonets were fixed and their rifles ready, and disappeared into their thoughts. In those last minutes, though the battlefield might teem with 200,000 men, every soldier was dreadfully, painfully alone.

If his generals were standing on the defensive, holding a good piece of ground, the soldier's first sight of the battlefield might have been from behind a farmer's rail or stone fence, a hastily dug rifle pit, or log and earth breastworks. Once there, he had more waiting in store. First the enemy's artillery would open up on his position, trying to blast his defenses with solid shot, or disrupt the formations manning it with exploding shells. Sitting out the barrage, the man knew that it was only the prelude

BELOW: A black fighting man of the famous 54th Massachusetts Infantry, one of the fortunate survivors of the bloody July 1863 assault on Fort Wagner, South Carolina. He and others settled the question of whether the black would fight.

to the enemy's charge. In a few minutes – though sometimes not until after an hour of shelling – the cannon fell silent and the foe appeared, rank by rank, in the distance, bayonets gleaming, flags fluttering, and all sporadically seen through the pall of gunsmoke that hung low and sluggish over the field. Bugles and shouts announced the charge, and then the sight of them running toward him, throats lustily giving forth their battle cries, while his own artillery behind him opened up with case-shot and canister, trying to break up the charge before it reached the works. Seeing several thousand screaming men rushing toward him, a soldier could feel very solitary indeed.

If he were on the other side, however, the story was different, and in a way easier. At least there he was not sitting through the shelling, not looking over the field to see the masses arrayed against him. He felt a part of the mass as his regiment, brigade, division, or even corps, marshalled its ranks for the charge. Fear was forgotten in the rush to get everything ready. There was no time in these last moments for anything but remembering what he was supposed to do. Then came the bugles and

drums, the swaggering officers, the anxious hush along the line, and the order to go.

Contrary to popular mythology, very few combats ever came down to hand-to-hand fighting, and bayonets inflicted so few wounds on an enemy as to be virtually worthless. An indefinable moment came in an attack when one side or the other flinched first. Most assaults failed, thanks to the power that rifled weapons gave to well-placed defenders, and the shock value of thundering artillery backing up the defenders. When an attack succeeded, it generally did so – as at Missionary Ridge in November 1863 – by the defenders being psychologically beaten by the sight of what was coming towards them, and abandoning their position before the enemy actually arrived. In time the men learned this. They also learned to keep their eyes straight ahead, to worry about seemingly mundane things like the rocks on the ground before them, not stumbling, and keeping close to the rest of the men in their lines.

FACING PAGE: Battle as boys fancied it before going to war. The reality proved to be a rude awakening when it came – all confusion, smoke and noise, with little of the glorious.

Of course, no man could shut his eyes to the horrors taking place around him. "I have Seen," one Yankee wrote home, "men rolling in their own blood." "They lay mangled and torn to pieces so that Even friends could not tell them." A Georgia boy confessed the "you doant know what kind of a-feeling it put on me to see men shot down like hoges & See a man tore all to peases with a Shell after he is dead." And for those who were really active in the slaughter, the effect could be even more traumatic. "I shot men," confessed a Mississippian, "until my heart was sick at the slaughter."

ABOVE: For more than half a million, this is what the war came to, death in a muddy Petersburg trench, a hospital, or a prison camp. TOP: The "fortunate" ones at least went to their final rest with their names. Thousands would be listed simply as "unknown" to posterity.

ABOVE: A typical Yankee outfit, Company C of the 110th Pennsylvania Infantry, shows the youthful, sometimes shambling, sometimes erect, face that Rebs and Yanks alike turned to their foe in some 10,000 engagements large and small. Some were heroes, some were cowards, most were simply patriots caught up in the greatest event of their time.

Then it was over. Such scenes might be repeated a dozen times in a day, for two or three days running in a major battle, but at last came the moment when one side or the other quit the field, or both armies simply sat down and stared at each other, too weary to fight on. The physical and emotional let-down was profound. "I did not know how tired I was until the excitement of the battle was over," wrote a Minnesota boy after the Battle of Gaines' Mill in June 1862. "I was almost too weak to stand, and my cheeks as hollow as though emaciated by a long spell of sickness." He collapsed under a bush "and slept such a sleep as comes only to a tired soldier after a battle."

Heroism was a relative term in the Civil War. Few distinguished themselves above their fellows for heroism, and yet any man who could stand up to the horrors of the battlefield, and the terrors in his own heart, was a hero of sorts if he did not turn and flee. In fact, of course, there were heroes a-plenty, caused as much by circumstance, luck and accident as by any conscious design. In the Union, the War Department in 1862 established the Medal of Honor. It was awarded both to honor those who stretched themselves beyond what was normally expected of a soldier in the face of the enemy, as well as to provide an incentive to others, a source of pride to men and regiments and families back

home. Jefferson Davis, too, authorized a Confederate Medal of Honor, but it was never issued, and instead men who distinguished themselves had their names added to a "Roll of Honor" that was read aloud to the armies after battles and published in the press. One actual medal was awarded, to a tiny band of defenders of the fort at Sabine Pass, Texas, when a silver dollar was milled flat and inscribed with the name of the action.

The war taught the soldiers blue and gray a valuable lesson in an era not noted for its tolerance. Heroism came in all colors and nationalities. Irish, German, Polish, Protestant, Catholic, Jew, white, black, or red, men in battle behaved the same. Several thousand American Indians served in each army, and many distinguished themselves, adding heroism to other notable attributes like names such as Jumper Duck, George Hogtotoer, Big Mush Dirt Eater, and more. Mexican-Americans, too, served in the armies, especially in the Confederate service under officers like Refugio Benavides. And some 180,000 free blacks and former slaves donned the Union blue. Most never saw real action, but when they did, as with the spectacular, doomed attack of the 54th Massachusetts on Battery Wagner in July 1863, they proved that, whether skin was white or black, blood was only red, and valor knew no color.

ABOVE: One thing that experience at war did not change was the devotion of soldiers to their regimental banners; men literally died protecting their colors, or proudly vied for the opportunity to carry them aloft in the forefront of battle, as in this Union charge during the Battle of Cold Harbor, Virginia on June I, 1864. The color-bearer's was the shortest life expectancy in the outfit. **LEFT:** Rebel cavalry carry the Confederate "battleflag" with the same reverence that they devoted to it for generations after the war.

CREDITS TO ILLUSTRATIONS
The publishers wish to thank the following individuals and organizations for granting permission to
reproduce the illustrations used in this book:
The Bettmann Archive; Bevoir-Jefferson Davis; Civil War Museum and Library;
Confederate Memorial Hall, New Orleans; Kentucky Historical Library; John Henry Kurtz;
Library of Congress; Missouri Historical Society; Museum of the Confederacy; National Archives;
Don Troiani; Bill Turner; U.S. Military Historical Institute, Carlisle, PA; Virginia State Archives

ABOVE: In the end it was the friendships made and the
simple, quiet moments that the soldiers remembered
and treasured most of all.